MW00425844

ENDORSEMENTS

"Jeffrey Brooks is a man who has been both a Marine and in the Army. His skills accompanied by his servant heart make him the right man to pen this book. I feel that it will even reach further than he thinks. I can see coaches giving this to some of the players in the NFL or NBA. I am proud to support this book and Jeffrey Brooks."

DWAYNE FOSTER,
PRESIDENT & CEO,
STINSON PRESS, INC.

"Our nation is exceptional because of the core values that regulate the lives of our citizens. Our Soldiers carry those values with them wherever they go in our country and around the world. One of those key values is a man's spirit, . . . for as is his spirit, so are the truths in his life. Chaplain Brooks' book of encouragement for those young men and women in boot camp illustrates his concern and love of them in training, as well as his quest to provide each with the elements of strength and courage needed for them to be the individuals their buddies will require on the battlefields of life they will experience. The core values of faith accompanying them at enlistment, or acquired in boot camp . . . perhaps for the first time in their lives . . . will have as much, if not more, to do with their success as Soldiers than anything else they may encounter. Thanks, Chaplain Brooks, for your simple down-to-earth, thoughtful, and realistic approach to the spirit of our men and women in boot camp that can accompany them wherever they may go and help them recall their deity's past presence with them. May your efforts touch their lives and inspire their faith's deity with a permanent presence in the hearts of each."

COLONEL LUTHER R. (LUKE) LLOYD,
USA (RETIRED) AIRBORNE
INFANTRY, ARMOR AND MILITARY
INTELLIGENCE PROFESSIONAL

"Throughout a service member's career, they are going to learn a lot about the development and use of resiliency—building mental, physical, emotional, behavioral and spiritual strength to enhance their ability to manage the rigors and challenges of a demanding profession. Chaplain Brooks' knowledge and experience has rightly identified that this development needs to begin in boot camp or basic combat training. These young men and women have volunteered to serve their nation and are transitioning into Soldiers, Sailors, Airmen, and Marines. *Resting in God's Shadow* inspires them to maintain a positive attitude and to never give up on themselves or their dreams in spite of the challenges they face, and throughout it all to give their very best."

PATRICK D QUINN III,
COLONEL, US ARMY

"Finished your book and I think you are right on; it should provide encouragement to those in any military boot camp, or life in general, and struggling to get through the change from civilian to military life. For some it is easy; for others the change is traumatic and they need encouragement."

LCDR John Glynn
OF GLYNSTEWART,
OST.J, FSA SCOT, MBA, USN (RET.)

"Chaplain Brooks is a combat-experienced, well-trained Army chaplain who is dedicated to caring for fellow service members. As a commander in combat, I witnessed his desire to help Soldiers and assist them through numerous emotionally and spiritually difficult times. These devotionals are designed to help all initial entry military trainees adapt to and overcome new challenges presented to them with their decision to serve."

Sonja Granger Dyer,
LIEUTENANT COLONEL,
US ARMY

RESTING
IN
GOD'S
SHADOW

ENCOURAGEMENT FOR
MILITARY BOOT CAMP

"I've been there, and I understand."

JEFFREY L. BROOKS

Resting in God's Shadow: Encouragement for Military Boot Camp
Copyright © 2017 by Jeffrey Brooks
Published by Deep River Books
Sisters, Oregon
www.deepriverbooks.com

No part of this book may be reproduced or transmitted in any form or by any means, electronic or mechanical, including photocopying and recording, or by any information storage and retrieval system, without permission in writing from the publisher.

Scripture quotations are from THE HOLY BIBLE, NEW INTERNATIONAL VERSION®, NIV® Copyright © 1973, 1978, 1984, 2011 by Biblica, Inc.® Used by permission. All rights reserved worldwide.

ISBN – 13: 9781632694317
Library of Congress: 2017930746

Printed in the USA

Cover design by Joe Bailen

DEDICATION

I want to dedicate this book to the men and women in boot camp, who have chosen to serve and defend our nation.

CONTENTS

PART TWO
A Boot Camp Prayer Book

Jeffrey L. Brooks

INTRODUCTION

Two things that I will never forget about my experience while in Marine Corps boot camp were the emotion that I felt when I arrived, and the emotion that I felt when I graduated. Something that I learned about boot camp was that if I took one day at time and gave it my best, everything would work out fine.

The same is true for you. If you will hang in there and give it your best, everything will work out fine for you.

After serving in the Marines for seven years, I went to college. In 1989, I earned my bachelor of arts degree and completed the Army ROTC program. Then in 2002, I graduated from the US Army Chaplaincy School and served as a chaplain until I retired in 2013.

One of the high points of my Army chaplaincy was serving as boot camp chaplain at Fort Leonard Wood, Missouri. Every day, I listened to and encouraged young men and women in boot camp. I have heard every frustration trainees experience that you can imagine. In fact, that is the reason I wrote this book. I have been there, and I understand.

While you are in boot camp, I want you to remember: Never give up on yourself or your dreams; keep a positive mental attitude; and give your very best each day. This is very important. If you hang in there and give it your best, everything will work out fine.

I want to devote a few lines now to introduce the book itself. This book is a collection of twelve devotionals, followed by a prayer book with spaces to record your thoughts. The devotionals in Part One correspond with the prayer book in Part Two. If you want to get the most out of this book, here's what I recommend: After reading each devotional, turn to the corresponding section in Part Two, so that you can record and keep track of your prayers.

In writing this book, I have done my best—to bring out *your* best, during boot camp! I wish you the very best. God bless you!

PART ONE

A Collection of Boot Camp Devotionals

1

NEVER GIVE UP

Has there ever been a time when you felt like you didn't know where you would find the strength you needed to keep going in life? Maybe you've felt like quitting, or as if it was time to give up on yourself or your dreams.

I will never forget something that my drill instructor shouted during a road march when I was in Marine Corps boot camp. At the exact moment I felt like I had nothing more left in me, he yelled, "Just take one more step and keep moving. When you trip and fall, you've got to get back up and keep moving because we need you and we've all got to finish this course and get back home together."

There will be times in boot camp when you will feel like you don't have the strength you need to keep going, and the thought of giving up and quitting might cross your mind. Promise yourself that when those times come, you will just take one more step and keep moving.

Never give up on yourself or your dreams. When you trip and fall, you've got to get back up and keep moving because we need you and we've all got to finish this course and get back home together. Will you?

I can do all this through him who gives me strength (Phil. 4:13).

****

Where does it seem hard to take that next step right now?

On the other hand, when have you taken that next step, even when you didn't think you had it in you? What happened?

Write your answers, and any other thoughts this devotional has sparked, in the space below.

_____

_____

_____

_____

_____

_____

_____

_____

_____

_____

_____

_____

_____

_____

_____

_____

_____

_____

_____

_____

_____

_____

_____

_____

_____

_____

_____

_____

_____

_____

_____

2

IF I COULD HAVE KNOWN

Have you ever thought, "If I had only known yesterday what was coming down the road for me today, I would have done things differently"?

When I was a child, my parents took me to New York City to see the Macy's Thanksgiving Day Parade. The spectators, tall to a young boy and standing shoulder-to-shoulder in front of me to keep warm, blocked my view. My dad lifted me up, and suddenly, I was high enough above the crowd to see the balloons, floats, bands, and performers as they came down the road toward us. I could now see what was coming down the road.

The Bible tells us that God is high enough above that He can see what is coming down the road toward us during boot camp—and during every part of our lives. God sees what we are facing today, and He sees what we will face tomorrow. He knows what's coming, even when you don't.

I want to encourage you to pause as you go to sleep each evening and ask God to bless what is coming toward you tomorrow. Ask God to give you wisdom and strength for what is ahead of you, each day, as you approach graduation. Will you?

Great is our Lord and mighty in power; his understanding has no limit (Ps. 147:5).

****

When have you thought, "If I had only known yesterday what was coming down the road for me today, I would have done things differently?"

What do you wish you knew right now?

How can trusting God help you further down the road, even if you don't know what's coming next—or even if you do?

Write your answers, and any other thoughts, in the space below. Be sure also to record any prayer requests in Part 2 of this book.

_____

_____

_____

_____

_____

_____

_____

_____

_____

_____

_____

_____

_____

_____

_____

_____

_____

_____

_____

_____

_____

_____

_____

_____

_____

_____

_____

_____

3

CHALLENGES, STRUGGLES, AND ANXIETIES

The Bible says, "Humble yourselves, therefore, under God's mighty hand, that he may lift you up in due time. Cast all your anxiety on him because he cares for you" (1 Pet. 5:6–7). God is in the business of lifting us up. He wants to help us, and He doesn't mind us asking for His help. What is the biggest problem you're facing that you can give to God today?

Did you know there is someone in boot camp who is there to lift you up and encourage you? Your chaplain is there to help you with your challenges, struggles, and anxieties. When I was a boot camp chaplain at Fort Leonard Wood, I enjoyed sitting down and talking with Soldiers about their concerns. Basic trainees asked for appointments to meet with me to talk about every frustration that you can imagine. I remember on one occasion, a Soldier asked to meet with me to pray with him about his relationship with his father. I have prayed with trainees about families, conflict with other trainees, medical concerns, upcoming tests, and more.

Have you ever had a time in your life when you needed to find someone safe to talk with? Maybe you would like to meet with a person who is good at listening. Believe it or not, that's what chaplains are here for. We are here to listen to you. Your chaplain is here to help you get from where you are today to where you want to be tomorrow!

When you get frustrated and don't know what to do, ask for an appointment with your chaplain. We're good listeners.

I want to encourage you to speak with your chaplain while in basic training if you need someone to lift you up and encourage you. We don't mind you asking for our help. Will you?

****

Again, what's the biggest problem you're facing that you can give to God today?

What, if anything, holds you back from seeking help or counsel from your chaplain?

Write your answers, and any other reactions to this devotional, in the space below.

_____

_____

_____

_____

_____

_____

_____

_____

_____

_____

_____

_____

_____

_____

_____

_____

_____

_____

_____

_____

_____

_____

_____

_____

_____

_____

_____

_____

_____

_____

_____

_____

LET GO AND FORGIVE

Have you ever had a time in your life when it was hard to let go and forgive someone who upset you? I know I have. Forgiving people is not something that comes naturally to me. When it comes to people who upset me, being bitter and resentful comes naturally.

Several years ago, a book at Fort Leonard Wood got my attention. It was about the physical, emotional, and spiritual benefits that come to people who learn how to forgive others. The words written in that book had such a strong influence on me that I did something I wouldn't have normally done: I asked for help. I asked someone to help me learn how to forgive people.

Asking someone to help me learn to forgive was the best thing I could have done for myself. I'm glad I did it. Nothing good comes from holding on to bitterness and resentment.

Who is it that you need to forgive today? Do you need to forgive someone with whom you are training? Maybe you need to forgive a family member. I want to encourage you to make it a point to be forgiving during boot camp. Learning to forgive people has made a difference in my life, and I think that it can make a difference in your life, too. I hope you will join me in choosing to be forgiving. Will you?

Be kind and compassionate to one another, forgiving each other, just as in Christ God forgave you (Eph. 4:32).

****

How have you seen the effects of unforgiveness in your life?

Who do you need to forgive right now? Who can help you to forgive?

Write your answers in the space below, and be sure to add your answers to the second question to your prayer requests in Part 2 of this book.

_____

_____

_____

_____

_____

_____

_____

_____

_____

_____

_____

_____

_____

_____

_____

_____

_____

_____

_____

_____

_____

_____

_____

_____

_____

_____

_____

_____

_____

_____

_____

5

MAIL CALL AND WHAT MATTERS MOST

When I was in Iraq a few years ago, someone said, "Chaplain, I'd give anything in the world to be with my family today. I'd give anything in the world to be able to hug my two little daughters this year for Christmas."

Those of us in the military are in such a hurry that it's easy for us to miss out on enjoying the company of our families and friends, which is what matters most. I want to encourage you to slow down and make a point of spending quality time with your family and friends after graduation. Be sure to hug your family members and those close to you as soon as you graduate and see them. Don't be in such a hurry while you are in the military that you forget about what matters the most.

One of the best ways to keep in touch with family and friends during boot camp is by sending postcards. During boot camp, you can purchase letter-writing material at the PX (post exchange) or BX (base exchange). Likewise, be sure to ask friends and family to send you plenty of letters while you're in training. Let people know that you *want* to get mail from them. Don't forget to take your address book with you to basic training and send a postcard during your first week of training to everyone you can think of. Will you?

****

Who do you miss the most back home? What would you like to tell him or her right now?

In addition, who could encourage you and give you good advice during your time in boot camp? Which do you need more?

Write your answers, and any other thoughts this devotional has sparked, in the space below.

_____

_____

_____

_____

_____

_____

_____

_____

_____

_____

_____

_____

_____

_____

_____

_____

_____

_____

_____

_____

_____

_____

_____

_____

_____

_____

_____

_____

_____

_____

_____

6

LIGHTEN UP ON YOURSELF

Brothers and sisters, I do not consider myself yet to have taken hold of it. But one thing I do: Forgetting what is behind and straining toward what is ahead... (Phil. 3:13).

When reading the Bible, you are bound to notice that God used a lot of imperfect people to accomplish a lot of great things in the world. Have you ever had the unbiblical thought that God could never use you to make a difference in the world because of your shortcomings and past failures?

In the passage above, the apostle Paul says that while he knows he had plenty of shortcomings and failures in the past, he would not let them keep him from being his very best today. Paul learned how to lighten up on himself, let go of the past, and do a lot of significant things while he was alive. He didn't let his past failures keep him from being his very best.

Do you realize how much positive difference you can make in the lives of those you encounter each day, even while you're in boot camp? The truth is, none of us are perfect. Don't let your imperfections keep you from being your very best and making a difference in the world.

Find one specific thing you can do each day that will have a positive influence on those with whom you are training. It is not difficult. For example, you can simply encourage others and keep a positive attitude. We all need positive people in our lives to encourage us. Why can't it be you?

I challenge you to be a person who encourages others in boot camp. Encourage people, keep a positive attitude, and give your very best to boot camp. Will you?

****

Do you feel like your shortcomings and past failures hold you back today? If so, how? How does God's Word help you to know that this isn't true?

How can you positively influence others today, and in the days to come?

Write your answers in the space below, and add any prayer requests this devotional has inspired in Part 2 of this book.

_____

_____

_____

_____

_____

_____

_____

_____

_____

_____

_____

_____

_____

_____

_____

_____

_____

_____

_____

_____

_____

_____

_____

_____

_____

_____

_____

_____

7

THE BEST THING YOU CAN DO

Several years ago, while stationed at Fort Leonard Wood, my doctor told me that I had the signs and symptoms of sleep deprivation. He said that the best thing I could do for myself was to always get a good night's sleep.

One of the most valuable things I have learned in life is the importance of getting a good night's sleep. There is a relationship between the sleep we get and our physical, mental, emotional, and spiritual well-being.

I encourage you to try your best to get a good night's sleep while you are in boot camp, so that you can wake up each morning well rested. If you want to get the best *from* yourself while you're awake, you need to get the best *for* yourself while you're asleep. People who get the rest they need do much better than people who don't. The best thing that you can do for yourself during boot camp is to make sure to always get a good night's sleep. Will you?

Come to me, all you who are weary and burdened, and I will give you rest. Take my yoke upon you and learn from me, for I am gentle and humble in heart, and you will find rest for your souls (Matt. 11:28–29).

****

What, if anything, prevents you from getting a good night's sleep?

What changes do you need to make in either your thinking or you outward habits, so that you have the opportunity to get sufficient rest each night?

Write your answers, and anything else you've thought of while reading this devotional, in the space below.

_____

_____

_____

_____

_____

_____

_____

_____

_____

_____

_____

_____

_____

_____

_____

_____

_____

_____

_____

_____

_____

_____

_____

_____

_____

_____

_____

_____

_____

8

ARE YOU RUNNING ON EMPTY?

Have you ever found yourself driving your car on an empty tank of gas? A few years ago, while I was an Army chaplain at Fort Knox, I did just that. All of the sudden, while driving south toward Nashville, the "low-fuel warning" light started flashing on my dashboard. At that exact moment, I was not longer concerned about the high price of gas. What I was concerned about at that moment was finding a gas station, at any price, where I could pull off the road and fill my tank. I would have gladly paid double to refill my empty tank that day.

Something I've learned about myself is that if I don't make it a point to pull off the road occasionally to refill my tank—physically, emotionally, and spiritually—my engine stops running like it should. One of the best things I've learned to do is to find one or two places to pause and "pull off the road" each day to fill up my tank and take care of myself.

While you are in boot camp, I want to encourage you to look for some ways to fill up your tank and take care of yourself. One way to do this is by developing supportive relationships with those around you. Other ways to refuel and take care of yourself include attending chapel services, spending time in God's Word, or scheduling an appointment to talk and pray with your chaplain.

Make it a point to pull off the road occasionally to fill up your tank while you're in boot camp. If you do, I can guarantee you'll feel better and notice that it makes a difference in your life. Will you?

The thief comes only to steal and kill and destroy; I have come that they may have life, and have it to the full (John 10:10).

****

What tends to "drain your tank" the most?

How will you take the time to refuel each day? What changes do you need to make in your routine so that this is possible?

Write your answers, and any other thoughts that have come to you through this devotional, in the space below. Also be sure to add your prayer requests in Part 2 of this book, as needed.

_____

_____

_____

_____

_____

_____

_____

_____

_____

_____

_____

_____

_____

_____

_____

_____

_____

_____

_____

_____

_____

_____

_____

_____

_____

_____

_____

_____

_____

9

A SAFE PLACE DURING THE STORM

When I was just six years old, a tornado came through our small Indiana town and destroyed a lot of homes. I will never forget watching my father as he invited the neighbors to stay with us in our basement where it was safe. Everyone made it through without harm that night, because we had found a safe place to stay during the storm.

The same is true when it comes to the storms you will face during boot camp. Are you ready for them? Are you staying close to God, where it's safe? I hope you are.

You and I need to get close to God today, so that we can face the storms life brings tomorrow. Stay close to God where it's safe. Make it a point to get close to God today, before you're hit by rough weather and it's too late.

Do you need to make some room in your life for God? God has made a difference in my life, as both a Marine and a Soldier, and He can make a difference in your life if you let Him. I hope you will make room for God in your life while you are training in boot camp. Will you?

Come near to God and he will come near to you (James 4:8).

****

Do you make a point of drawing close to God in every circumstance, or do you usually wait until the storms come? Explain.

How can you make more room in your life for God right now, no matter how things are going for you?

Write your answers, and any other thoughts this devotional has stirred up, in the space below.

_____

_____

_____

_____

_____

_____

_____

_____

_____

_____

_____

_____

_____

_____

_____

_____

_____

_____

_____

_____

_____

_____

_____

_____

_____

_____

_____

_____

10

STAY CONNECTED LIKE YOU SHOULD

One cold winter morning, while I was serving as chaplain at Tobyhanna Army Depot, my car wasn't running at its best, so I asked my mechanic to take a look at it. As soon as he lifted the hood, he pointed to the engine and told me that the source of my problem was a disconnected hose. He added that as long as I took the time to make sure everything under the hood stayed connected as it should, my engine would keep running as it should.

I have learned that if I want my emotional, mental, and physical engines to run like they should, I must take time to make sure I stay connected with people who encourage me and who bring out the best in me. How about you? Are you staying connected with people who encourage you and bring out your best?

Be sure to make friends and connect with the other trainees during boot camp. Be a blessing to them. More importantly: Stay connected to God like you should. Ask God to bless you and bring out your best. As long as everything under the hood stays connected like it should, your engine will keep running like it should.

I am the vine; you are the branches. If you remain in me and I in you, you will bear much fruit; apart from me you can do nothing (John 15:5).

****

How can you begin to connect better with both others and God?

How can you also be a blessing to others? Be specific.

Write your answers, and any other connections you've made while reading this devotional, in the space below.

_____

_____

_____

_____

_____

_____

_____

_____

_____

_____

_____

_____

_____

_____

_____

_____

_____

_____

_____

_____

_____

_____

_____

_____

_____

_____

_____

_____

_____

_____

_____

_____

11

RESTING IN GOD'S SHADOW

I enjoy watching the ducklings rest in the shadows of the trees surrounding my backyard pond. Whenever I watch them, I'm reminded of a Bible passage I used to share with our military men and women in Iraq: "Whoever dwells in the shelter of the Most High will rest in the shadow of the Almighty. I will say of the Lord, 'He is my refuge and my fortress, my God, in whom I trust'" (Ps. 91:1–2).

I believe the most significant word in this passage is "trust." If we want to have a trusting relationship with God while in boot camp, we have to open the door of our hearts and talk to Him.

In chapter 3 of the book of Revelation, Jesus says, "Here I am! I stand at the door and knock. If anyone hears my voice and opens the door, I will come in" (Rev. 3:20). I want to encourage you to open the door of your heart and rest in God's protective shadow. When you get a break in training, take some time to pray, and ask God to bless you. (And again, write your prayers in the back of this book, and watch what God does with them.) Keep a positive attitude, and ask God to give you the strength you need to give your very best during boot camp. Will you?

****

In what ways do you struggle with trusting God?

Where could you use some "shadow"? In other words: Where do you need to open the door to God right now?

Write your answers, and any other ideas this devotional has opened up, in the space below.

_____

_____

_____

_____

_____

_____

_____

_____

_____

_____

_____

_____

_____

_____

_____

_____

_____

_____

_____

_____

_____

_____

_____

_____

_____

_____

_____

_____

_____

_____

_____

_____

12

"IF I COULD GET HIM TO TALK"

Several years ago, I heard a wife say, "If I could get him to talk to me, it would make a big difference in our married life." The key to a good relationship with a person's spouse is good communication.

In the same way, the key to a good relationship with your Lord is good communication. Your spiritual life can become so much better just by talking to God. If you want God to make a difference in your life, you've got to make an investment in your relationship with Him and start talking.

The Bible says, "Do not be anxious about anything, but in every situation, by prayer and petition, with thanksgiving, present your requests to God. And the peace of God, which transcends all understanding, will guard your hearts and your minds in Christ Jesus" (Phil. 4:6–7).

How much of an investment do you make in your relationship with God? One way to invest in your relationship with God, during boot camp, is by keeping a written record of your prayers. This is something that I did as a chaplain and I continue to do. I've found this to be one of the most helpful suggestions that I have given to young men and women who are in boot camp.

The next section of this book is provided so that you can keep a written record of your prayers during boot camp; hopefully you've already started using the pages there. Call it your Boot Camp Prayer Book. I want to encourage you to keep connected to God by writing down what you are praying about on the pages that follow. Will you?

****

What do you need to say to God right now? Write it in the space below. Then, move on to the introduction to the Boot Camp Prayer Book (Part 2).

_____

_____

_____

_____

_____

_____

_____

_____

_____

_____

_____

_____

_____

_____

_____

_____

_____

_____

_____

_____

_____

_____

_____

_____

_____

_____

_____

_____

_____

_____

_____

_____

_____

_____

PART TWO

A Boot Camp Prayer Book

INTRODUCTION

The following pages provide space for you to keep a written record of your prayers during boot camp. I want to encourage you to keep connected to God by writing down what you pray about during training on the pages that follow.

Please take some time to look through this part of the book, in its entirety, before you start. The twelve sections that follow correspond to the twelve devotionals in part one. Just as you did in Part One, you'll explore issues of strength and endurance, family, forgiveness, and other challenges you face every day in boot camp—and beyond. The last portion of this prayer book provides space for you to record prayers that might not fit into the first eleven categories.

Keeping a written record of my prayers is a discipline that I did as a chaplain, and it is a discipline that I continue to practice. Recording and tracking my prayers, like this, has made a big difference in my life, as I see God's faithfulness in answering them. My prayer is that this practice will make a difference in your life, too.

PRAYERS FOR STRENGTH
TO FINISH WELL

I can do all this through him who gives me strength (Phil. 4:13).

Date Prayed & Prayer Concern

_____

_____

   Date Answered & Specifically How It Was Answered

   _____

   _____

   _____

Date Prayed & Prayer Concern

_____

_____

   Date Answered & Specifically How It Was Answered

   _____

   _____

   _____

Date Prayed & Prayer Concern

_____

_____

   Date Answered & Specifically How It Was Answered

   _____

   _____

   _____

Date Prayed & Prayer Concern

_____

_____

   Date Answered & Specifically How It Was Answered

   _____

   _____

   _____

Date Prayed & Prayer Concern

_____

_____

   Date Answered & Specifically How It Was Answered

   _____

   _____

   _____

2

PRAYERS FOR GOD'S HELP IN UNDERSTANDING AND PASSING DAILY CLASSES

Great is our Lord and mighty in power; his understanding has no limits (Ps. 147:5).

Date Prayed & Prayer Concern

_____

_____

Date Answered & Specifically How It Was Answered

_____

_____

_____

Date Prayed & Prayer Concern

_____

_____

Date Answered & Specifically How It Was Answered

_____

_____

Date Prayed & Prayer Concern

_____

_____

    Date Answered & Specifically How It Was Answered

    _____

    _____

    _____

Date Prayed & Prayer Concern

_____

_____

    Date Answered & Specifically How It Was Answered

    _____

    _____

    _____

Date Prayed & Prayer Concern

_____

_____

    Date Answered & Specifically How It Was Answered

    _____

    _____

    _____

3

PRAYERS FOR SPECIFIC PROBLEMS AND DIFFICULTIES

Humble yourselves, therefore, under God's mighty hand, that he may lift you up in due time. Cast all your anxiety on him because he cares for you (1 Pet. 5:6–7).

Date Prayed & Prayer Concern

_____

_____

Date Answered & Specifically How It Was Answered

_____

_____

_____

Date Prayed & Prayer Concern

_____

_____

Date Answered & Specifically How It Was Answered

_____

_____

Date Prayed & Prayer Concern

_____

_____

    Date Answered & Specifically How It Was Answered

    _____

    _____

    _____

Date Prayed & Prayer Concern

_____

_____

    Date Answered & Specifically How It Was Answered

    _____

    _____

    _____

Date Prayed & Prayer Concern

_____

_____

    Date Answered & Specifically How It Was Answered

    _____

    _____

    _____

PRAYERS FOR THE PEOPLE I NEED TO LEARN TO FORGIVE

Be kind and compassionate to one another, forgiving each other, just as in Christ God forgave you (Eph. 4:32).

Date Prayed & Prayer Concern

_____

_____

    Date Answered & Specifically How It Was Answered

    _____

    _____

    _____

Date Prayed & Prayer Concern

_____

_____

    Date Answered & Specifically How It Was Answered

    _____

    _____

Date Prayed & Prayer Concern

_____

_____

Date Answered & Specifically How It Was Answered

_____

_____

_____

Date Prayed & Prayer Concern

_____

_____

Date Answered & Specifically How It Was Answered

_____

_____

_____

Date Prayed & Prayer Concern

_____

_____

Date Answered & Specifically How It Was Answered

_____

_____

_____

PRAYERS FOR MY FAMILY

This is the confidence we have in approaching God: that if we ask anything according to his will, he hears us. And if we know that he hears us—whatever we ask—we know that we have what we asked of him (2 John 5:14–15).

Date Prayed & Prayer Concern

_____

_____

    Date Answered & Specifically How It Was Answered

    _____

    _____

    _____

Date Prayed & Prayer Concern

_____

_____

    Date Answered & Specifically How It Was Answered

    _____

    _____

Date Prayed & Prayer Concern

_____

_____

Date Answered & Specifically How It Was Answered

_____

_____

_____

Date Prayed & Prayer Concern

_____

_____

Date Answered & Specifically How It Was Answered

_____

_____

_____

Date Prayed & Prayer Concern

_____

_____

Date Answered & Specifically How It Was Answered

_____

_____

_____

PRAYERS FOR SELF-FORGIVENESS
(LIGHTENING UP ON MYSELF)

Brothers and sisters, I do not consider myself yet to have taken hold of it. But one thing I do: Forgetting what is behind and straining toward what is ahead . . . (Phil. 3:13).

Date Prayed & Prayer Concern

_____

_____

   Date Answered & Specifically How It Was Answered

_____

_____

_____

Date Prayed & Prayer Concern

_____

_____

   Date Answered & Specifically How It Was Answered

_____

_____

Date Prayed & Prayer Concern

_____

_____

Date Answered & Specifically How It Was Answered

_____

_____

_____

Date Prayed & Prayer Concern

_____

_____

Date Answered & Specifically How It Was Answered

_____

_____

_____

Date Prayed & Prayer Concern

_____

_____

Date Answered & Specifically How It Was Answered

_____

_____

_____

PRAYERS FOR REST—AND FOR A GOOD NIGHT'S SLEEP

Come to me, all you who are weary and burdened, and I will give you rest. Take my yoke upon you and learn from me, for I am gentle and humble in heart, and you will find rest for your souls (Matt. 11:28–29).

Date Prayed & Prayer Concern

_____

_____

Date Answered & Specifically How It Was Answered

_____

_____

_____

Date Prayed & Prayer Concern

_____

_____

Date Answered & Specifically How It Was Answered

_____

_____

Date Prayed & Prayer Concern

_____

_____

   Date Answered & Specifically How It Was Answered

   _____

   _____

   _____

Date Prayed & Prayer Concern

_____

_____

   Date Answered & Specifically How It Was Answered

   _____

   _____

   _____

Date Prayed & Prayer Concern

_____

_____

   Date Answered & Specifically How It Was Answered

   _____

   _____

   _____

8

PRAYERS TO BE UPLIFTED AND ENCOURAGED BY OTHERS

The thief comes only to steal and kill and destroy; I have come that they may have life, and have it to the full (John 10:10).

Date Prayed & Prayer Concern

_____

_____

   Date Answered & Specifically How It Was Answered

      _____

      _____

      _____

Date Prayed & Prayer Concern

_____

_____

   Date Answered & Specifically How It Was Answered

      _____

      _____

Date Prayed & Prayer Concern

_____

_____

    Date Answered & Specifically How It Was Answered

    _____

    _____

    _____

Date Prayed & Prayer Concern

_____

_____

    Date Answered & Specifically How It Was Answered

    _____

    _____

    _____

Date Prayed & Prayer Concern

_____

_____

    Date Answered & Specifically How It Was Answered

    _____

    _____

    _____

PRAYERS TO STAY SAFELY
CLOSE TO GOD

Come near to God and he will come near to you
(James 4:8).

Date Prayed & Prayer Concern

_____

_____

   Date Answered & Specifically How It Was Answered

   _____

   _____

   _____

Date Prayed & Prayer Concern

_____

_____

   Date Answered & Specifically How It Was Answered

   _____

   _____

Date Prayed & Prayer Concern

_____

_____

Date Answered & Specifically How It Was Answered

_____

_____

_____

Date Prayed & Prayer Concern

_____

_____ _____

Date Answered & Specifically How It Was Answered

_____

_____

_____

Date Prayed & Prayer Concern

_____

_____

Date Answered & Specifically How It Was Answered

_____

_____

_____

10

PRAYERS FOR OPPORTUNITIES TO CONNECT OTHERS TO GOD

I am the vine; you are the branches. If you remain in me and I in you, you will bear much fruit; apart from me you can do nothing (John 15:5).

Date Prayed & Prayer Concern

_____

_____

    Date Answered & Specifically How It Was Answered

_____

_____

_____

Date Prayed & Prayer Concern

_____

_____

    Date Answered & Specifically How It Was Answered

_____

_____

Date Prayed & Prayer Concern

_____

_____

   Date Answered & Specifically How It Was Answered

   _____

   _____

   _____

Date Prayed & Prayer Concern

_____

_____

   Date Answered & Specifically How It Was Answered

   _____

   _____

   _____

Date Prayed & Prayer Concern

_____

_____

   Date Answered & Specifically How It Was Answered

   _____

   _____

   _____

PRAYERS FOR GOD'S DAILY PROTECTION

Whoever dwells in the shelter of the Most High will rest in the shadow of the Almighty. I will say of the LORD, "HE IS MY REFUGE AND MY FORTRESS, MY GOD, IN WHOM I TRUST" (Ps. 91:1–2).

Date Prayed & Prayer Concern

———————————————————————————

———————————————————————————

 Date Answered & Specifically How It Was Answered

 ———————————————————————

 ———————————————————————

 ———————————————————————

Date Prayed & Prayer Concern

———————————————————————————

———————————————————————————

 Date Answered & Specifically How It Was Answered

 ———————————————————————

 ———————————————————————

Date Prayed & Prayer Concern

_____

_____

Date Answered & Specifically How It Was Answered

_____

_____

_____

Date Prayed & Prayer Concern

_____

_____

Date Answered & Specifically How It Was Answered

_____

_____

_____

Date Prayed & Prayer Concern

_____

_____

Date Answered & Specifically How It Was Answered

_____

_____

_____

12

PRAYERS FOR EVERY OTHER THING

Do not be anxious about anything, but in every situation, by prayer and petition, with thanksgiving, present your requests to God. And the peace of God, which transcends all understanding, will guard your hearts and your minds in Christ Jesus (Phil. 4:6–7).

Date Prayed & Prayer Concern

_____

_____

    Date Answered & Specifically How It Was Answered

    _____

    _____

    _____

Date Prayed & Prayer Concern

_____

_____

Wood, Missouri, where he was deployed to Iraq for twelve months, in support of Operation Iraqi Freedom. In June of 2005, he completed a year with the 1st Battalion, 15th Field Artillery, 2nd Infantry Division, Camp Hovey, South Korea.

Jeff graduated from the US Army Chaplain School Advanced Course in 2006. Afterward, he served as chaplaincy resource manager at Fort Knox, and then as brigade chaplain of the 3rd Chemical Brigade, Fort Leonard Wood, Missouri.

Jeff completed twenty-two years of active military service while serving as chaplain at Toby-hanna Army Depot, Pennsylvania. He retired in 2013 and now resides in Tampa, Florida.

Connect with the Author at:
mychaplain@yahoo.com